CONTENTMENT

BY
ANDRE RABE

ISBN: 978-0-9563346-0-2

Published by Andre Rabe Publishing.

Contents

INTRODUCTION

Young lions lie down in complete satisfaction after feasting on their prey. Despite their great strength, they have no greater ambition than satisfying their most basic natural cravings. Most animals are content with little more than food, but man has an appetite that seems insatiable. Mankind has a consciousness of value that drives us to explore every avenue, to push every limit, to tunnel through mountains, to build habitations in space, to invent a microscope like the Large Hadron Collider that is 27km long, to peer into the smallest detail of matter, in search of information ... meaning ... something that satisfies beyond mere survival.

Despite technological advances and the comforts of a modern age, man's appetite and search for contentment has not been diminished. We travel more, we eat more, we have more gadgets and comforts, and the world's information is at our fingertips. To pay for it all we work longer hours, live more complicated and demanding lives, but do these things bring us any closer to the secret of contentment?

In approximately 60 AD, a man under house arrest, bound by chains to a Roman soldier, wrote the following: "I have learned the secret of contentment, whatever my circumstances." In another letter he wrote: "As you read you will understand my insight into the mystery of Christ."

It is this secret, this mystery, that we explore in this book.

Perspective

Don't shuffle along, eyes to the ground, absorbed with the things right in front of you. Look up, and be alert to what is going on around Christ—that's where the action is. See things from his perspective.

Colossians 3:2 (MSG)

How we see ourselves in the context of eternity can either leave us with a sense of insignificance or with a sense of awe at the beauty and value of our lives far beyond the confines of our time on earth. If our lives had no greater meaning than the few decades we are alive, then a sense of utter insignificance would be the only rational response ... but there is something of eternal significance in man.

One of the first concepts I was taught in art was 'perspective'. The connections between objects, the distances between them and the particular point of view all contribute to a unique perspective. I soon learnt that one point of view can hide the beauty in a scene, while another can reveal it. Nowhere is perspective more important than when we look at ourselves. Identity can be defined as an individual's comprehension of him or herself as a separate entity.

In practical terms this means that people tend to see themselves within the context of certain cultures, races and social settings to mention but a few of the broader influences. Language and location can have a profound effect on people's view of themselves. There are obviously more personal influences such as relationships with friends and family, not to mention the effect that personal experience has upon us. The list goes on and on - we find security in seeing ourselves in the context of something familiar.

It's in the midst of this that Jesus reveals a dimension, a context called eternity, so broad and so different that it totally disorientates us. Every temporal reference we use to locate and identify ourselves is challenged by the revelation Christ brings. In fact He plainly says that unless we lose our lives - lose our sense of identity - we will never find our true identity. In Jesus we encounter a new context to our lives - a perspective in which the distance that we believed to be between us and God, is cancelled.

Eternity dwarfs both our greatest achievements and deepest disappointments to minuscule size. Yet despite the seeming meaninglessness of our lives when placed in this context it also reveals our true value, for there is a part of us which is not temporal. *"He has made everything beautiful in its time. Also, he has put eternity into man's heart, without which man cannot find out what God has done from the beginning to the end."* (Eccl 3:11 LIT) God has placed eternity in our hearts so that we can have access into realms beyond the here and now, beyond the temporal, beyond the material. Because we are eternal beings, questions regarding eternity stir within us. He is not offended when we ask about these great mysteries - He placed those questions in our hearts so that we would seek and find. These questions are in-built invitations from our eternal Origin to reach into the spirit realm and find Him there.

Narrowness of experience

Another aspect of perspective is that one can get so close to an object, that it obscures one's view from all else. For many, personal experience has become the ultimate authority and measure of truth - it is the only thing they'll believe or place any confidence in. But there are few things that can skew our perspective more than personal experience. Let me explain:

In my early childhood - I was about five years old - we moved into a new house. Most of these houses in South Africa had big back yards and these made ideal playgrounds for small boys. We called it a 'yard' instead of a garden because it wasn't really a neatly kept garden - it was more like a large enclosure. On the day we moved in I noticed something very tempting: the neighbour had a small orchard of mango trees in his back yard ... and I loved mangoes. My dad must have read my thoughts because at the moment I noticed these trees, he said to me: "Don't even think of going into the neighbour's yard - there is a vicious dog guarding the trees". That was a very disappointing piece of information as through the days and weeks that followed I witnessed the mango fruit ripening.

I often played in the back yard in the afternoons and felt terribly tempted by the ripe mangoes over the fence, however my fear of the vicious dog prevented me from even attempting to pick a mango. One afternoon, while playing, I became desperately 'hungry' and the fruit seemed particularly inviting. I nervously sneaked onto the fence at the far end of the yard to have a better look at the dog, but I couldn't see the dog anywhere. I took my chance and jumped over the fence, grabbed a couple of mangoes and jumped back into my own yard. They were delicious!

It did not take me long to realise that there was no dog! The moral of the story is not about temptation or repentance or anything deeply spiritual like that. The point is simply that my experience of hunger was real, my experience of fear was real, but these real experiences were based on the lie that I believed regarding a vicious dog. The moment I realised that there was no dog the fear disappeared ... and as a consequence so did the hunger. How many of our real experiences are based on lies? How different would our experiences be, if we believed differently?

The truth that Jesus introduces us to is of a much higher authority than our experience - it is a truth that is able to transform our experience. He wants to introduce us to a truth much broader than our narrow experiences.

"... my judgement would be true because I wouldn't make it out of the narrowness of my experience but in the largeness of the One who sent me, the Father." (John 8:16 MSG). If Jesus considered his own experience as narrow compared to a much greater reality, then we too might have to re-evaluate the importance we attach to personal experience.

In the same way as our personal experiences are to narrow to reveal our true identity, so too is our culture too narrow; our language too narrow; our society too narrow; our race too narrow; even our relationships, no matter how precious, are too narrow. He reveals that all the measures we've used to measure ourselves with are completely inadequate. "*but when they measure themselves by themselves and compare themselves with themselves, they are without understanding*" (2 Cor. 10:12). He shatters our illusions, but at that very moment He also brings to light the truth of our design. We are eternal beings, which means that anything temporal will not do justice to God's estimation of our worth and He invites us to see ourselves from His point of view.

What do you refer to, to describe yourself? Is it your family traits; your unique childhood; your achievements? Or maybe you have allowed some tragedy to become the defining event of who you are. There is a more valid reference! If you don't discover that reference, you will allow experiences to shape and twist you. But when you discover that your identity was established in eternity, no temporal event will have the power to deceive you anymore.

Come to this conclusion: I am more than the sum total of my experience. I am greater than all the events in my life joined together. I'm bigger than my biggest disappointment or achievement. I am the image and likeness of God and not a fraction of me has been revealed.

Another way in which a person can define themselves is by what they have gained or by what they have lost. Pride and regret are both deceptions, designed for the same purpose: to blind man; to keep man from seeing his true value, a value far beyond all the wealth you can attain; a value untouched by anything you have ever lost.

A whole new dimension

There's a lot of talk these days about extra dimensions. A scientific theory that has received much attention lately is called 'string theory' and suggests that there are many more dimensions than those we currently observe. If you are interested in that type of thing, I found this web-site very interesting: http://www.pbs.org/wgbh/nova/elegant/program.html.

When mankind discovered the atom, many thought that it was the smallest particle that matter consists of, but pretty soon we understood that an atom consists of protons, neutrons and electrons. But what are they made of? Further investigation unveiled quarks! But what are they made of? A central concept to string theory is that the smallest components of matter are small bits of energy vibrating like the strings on a violin. These vibrations form a cosmic symphony which is at the heart of all reality. In the same way as a violin can produce many variations of musical notes, these strings, vibrating at different frequencies, form all the fundamental particles of the reality we observe. Our universe is the beautiful symphony produced by the resonance of all these vibrating strings. I can't but see the significance of Heb 1:3 speaking of Christ " ... *upholding and sustaining and propelling the universe by His mighty word of power."* At the core of all reality is sound - the sound of God's voice that spoke creation into being - the Voice that never grows dim, but continues to sustain all existence.

As mentioned before, string theory also suggests the existence of additional dimensions. There is indeed another dimension referred to in the scriptures - a dimension that existed before time and space as we know it; before creation; before the existence of evil. In this eternal realm, the purpose, the course, the duration and final destination of time and space was planned in meticulous detail before it even began. What happened in this dimension is of direct consequence to your existence!

Paul wrote about this dimension or realm in a letter to the Ephesians: "*Praise be to the God and Father of our Lord Jesus Christ Who has blessed us in Christ with every spiritual blessing in the heavenly realm! He chose us, identified and named us as His own in Christ before the foundation of the world, that we should be set apart for Him and blameless in His sight, even above reproach, before Him in love. For He destined us to be revealed as His own children through Jesus Christ, in accordance with the purpose of His will."*

Before our milky way was formed, before our sun ignited, before Jupiter or Mars began their orbit, before the earth was able to support life … you were planned, identified and named for a very specific purpose. You predate the dinosaurs! You began way before your conception - you began in the mind of God. "*Your eyes saw my unformed substance, and in Your book all the days of my life were written before ever they took shape, when as yet there was none of them.*" (Ps. 139:16). It is this realm, this eternal dimension, that preserves the truth about you. In our temporal, time-bound realm there might be many events, circumstances and experiences that try to contradict the truth about you … but they are as shadows compared to the unchangeable truth that was decided before this world began and will remain the only truth after this world has come to an end.

Some of you might remember a movie called 'Never Ending Story'. In this movie a boy starts reading a very special book that draws him into an entirely different world from his own. The book doesn't, in the first instance, give advice or direction for his world. In fact the story draws him into a new world, entirely oblivious to his current world and seemingly unconnected. Only closer to the end, as the boy understands more of this new world and more about himself in this new context, does the connection with his 'real' world become clear.

In a sense this is what the scriptures want to do - open a door into an entirely new world - the world of God - a world which at first seems entirely different and unconnected to our own. The first priority of the scriptures is not to comment on your life, your subject, your idea, your doctrine or your world - it has much greater ambitions and purposes. Only once you have allowed yourself to be taken to this new world, and discovered yourself in the context of this new world, do the connections and implications for our world become clear. I can't help thinking of the song: 'A Whole New World'. Here are a few of the lyrics that fit this concept so well:

...A whole new world
A new fantastic point of view...

A whole new world
A dazzling place I never knew
But when I'm way up here
It's crystal clear
That now I'm in a whole new world with you
Now I'm in a whole new world with you

A whole new world
Don't you dare close your eyes
A hundred thousand things to see
Hold your breath - it gets better

I'm like a shooting star

I've come so far

I can't go back to where I used to be .....

God wants to be more than an accessory to your world. His message is greater than a comment on your life. The scriptures have more to offer than a feel-good inspirational thought to help you through the day. As we read the scriptures, be ready to be transported into an entirely different setting, confronted by entirely new ideas, and transformed into an entirely new person.

Apprehended

...I press on so that I may lay hold of that for which also I was laid hold of by Christ Jesus.

Paul the Apostle

What is this strange … yet familiar attraction
this awareness of Your person that draws me beyond myself
It's not a desire for pleasure or any type of reward
it's a hand upon my spirit that pulls me toward
a consciousness of our union
without distraction.

What will You say …
Where will You take me …
You are utterly unpredictable yet completely dependable
and I revel in this uncertain security.
Uncertain, because You continually surprise me.
Secure, because I'm at home in Your embrace.

The more intimate our acquaintance
the greater the intrigue
of Your boundless person and infinite mind.

Here I belong; here I will abide.
I found the secret of satisfaction
yet there remains this mysterious magnetism
to explore Your height and depth,
to open my spirit eyes as wide as You.

And as I experience a vision of Your greatness,
I expand beyond the narrow confines
of earthly logic and my natural mind

to perceive what cannot be understood

and know for certain what cannot be explained.

(by Andre Rabe)

What I want to declare to you is not a truth that, in the first place, you can comprehend or apprehend ... but a truth that apprehends you, comprehends you. This declaration is about creating an opportunity for the truth to get a grip on you. This declaration is at best the opening of a window which reveals a landscape, a sight far greater than can be comprehended at once. When God reveals Himself the inevitable response is awe ... adoration. If you think that you can take a hold of and possess what you see, then you haven't seen God - you've seen something far inferior.

If, in all we say, we simply inform one another, help one another to better order our concepts of God, then we have failed in our communication. The power of our testimony lies not in what we know, but in who knows us. "*...now that you know God—or rather are known by God*" (Gal 4:9). To know God is of immeasurable value, but there is something even more valuable, even more astounding: we are known by Him! I believe that this gospel is much more than an orderly human doctrine of God; this gospel is the power of God unto salvation. This gospel originates in the heart of God and both its declaration and the faith it stirs are gifts of God - not inventions of man.

It's so easy to settle for words that tickle our ears; words that confirm our beliefs or add useful information to our understanding of God. But this Gospel is much more likely to confront our conceptions of Him; to shake the foundations of our arguments and to take us beyond the comfort of the familiar - to reveal that which no eye has seen, no ear has heard nor has entered the mind of man. It is only once the false fortresses of our own concepts are destroyed, only once every high thought is brought down, that we can begin to sense the real meaning of this gospel; that we can begin to hear the deep calling unto deep - the echo of our hearts responding to His call.

He desires to reveal Himself, but before His Word can be the comforting voice of our Father, it needs to be the fearful sound of weapons of warfare. For just as Paul zealously persecuted Christians in the belief that he was serving God, so we can hold onto doctrines, arguments and principles in the belief that they serve God, not realising that these are the very thoughts that oppose His purpose in our lives.

He will not allow His words to be used to strengthen our deceptions - He will not speak comfort to our illusions. Many other words can be used to do this - our own interpretations of the Scriptures can be used to build our fortresses of comfort - our intellectual security - by which we convince ourselves that we have Him figured out; that we are in control; that we know just the principle to apply to get God to do what we need Him to do. He has no part in that. When He speaks, He shatters our illusions; He tears down every argument; He destroys every fortress. I'm so grateful He does, for it is far better to know that you are ignorant and consequently seek His enlightenment, than to live in the illusion that you are illuminated.

> Let Me now teach you
> how best to approach My Word:
>
> My Word is more than a comment on *your* thoughts,
> more than a reference to support *your* view,
> more than words to fill *your* mind,
> or quotes to support *your* philosophy.
>
> To grasp My thoughts, forsake your own!
> To have the mind of Christ, you have to lose you own!
> My Word is not a tame, fluffy pet you can control,
> it's a dangerous creature - devouring lesser words,
> destroying every argument, taking captive every thought.
>
> (by Andre Rabe)

Coming to the end of our own wisdom also marks the beginning of a new wisdom - a wisdom which does not have its origin in this world. God takes no delight in simply showing us the foolishness of our own wisdom, but brings us to this recognition for the greater purpose of making us receptive to His wisdom. This wisdom does not co-exist with any other wisdom

- all else is reduced to foolishness in its presence.

In Ephesians 3, Paul seems to be grappling for words to try and give a sense of the awesomeness of this love: "...exceedingly ... abundantly ... above all that we can ask ... or imagine". In verse 16 he starts by praying that we would be strengthened by His spirit in our inner man ... that we might be able to comprehend ... that which surpasses knowledge. This is a different kind of comprehension - an awareness that surpasses knowledge.

What makes Paul's writings so influential, so fascinating is not because he gives the impression that he has a broad and firm hold on the truth, but rather, the obvious fact that someone much greater than Paul had got a hold of him. In fact, in his letter to the Philippians he writes that his life's ambition is to try and get a hold of that which got a hold of him. "*I press on, that I may lay hold of that for which Christ Jesus has also laid hold of me.*" Phil 3:12

"*You'll remember, friends, that when I first came to you to let you in on God's master stroke, I didn't try to impress you with polished speeches and the latest philosophy. I deliberately kept it plain and simple: first Jesus and who he is; then Jesus and what he did—Jesus crucified.*

I was unsure of how to go about this, and felt totally inadequate—I was scared to death, if you want the truth of it—and so nothing I said could have impressed you or anyone else. But the Message came through anyway. God's Spirit and God's power did it, which made it clear that your life of faith is a response to God's power, not to some fancy mental or emotional footwork by me or anyone else.

We, of course, have plenty of wisdom to pass on to you once you get your feet on firm spiritual ground, but it's not popular wisdom, the fashionable wisdom of high-priced experts that will be out-of-date in a year or so. God's wisdom is something mysterious that goes deep into the interior of his purposes. You don't find it lying around on the surface. It's not the latest message, but more like the oldest—what God determined as the way to bring out his best in us, long before we ever arrived on the scene." 1 Cor 2:1-7

Revelation

But how do we receive this wisdom? This wisdom is not the product of our intellectual searching. In fact there is nothing we can do to attain it - it is completely hopeless! But precisely because we can do nothing to earn it, we are free to receive it as a gift - a gift which means that the initiative resides not with us but with the giver. He reveals Himself even to those who do not seek Him, proving that this message is not the product of enquiring minds or wishful thinking, but a truth that stands on its own whether we believe it or not, whether we seek it or not.

What no eye has seen, no ear has heard and has not entered the mind of man ... God revealed through His Spirit. God devised a way for us to see, what no eye has seen, to hear what no ear has heard, and to understand what no mind can conceive.

There have been events that I can't describe in any lesser terms than Divine encounters, in which God simply showed me something about Himself that forever changed who I was - or thought I was. It's as if He by-passed all of my intellect, all of my emotion and all of my imagination and displayed an image of Himself to my spirit. Like the shutter of a camera that opens and shuts in a millisecond yet is able to capture a scene of majestic and ancient beauty, so eternity exposed 'itself' to the temporal, the infinite to the finite.

These 'impressions', for lack of an adequate word, could take days, months or even years before they connect with my natural mind in order for me to articulate them accurately. It is as if my natural faculties have to race to keep up with an injection of perception that happened in a part so deep within me, that it is not immediately available to my mind. I have to draw it out as Proverbs says: "Counsel in the heart of man is like deep water; But a man of understanding will draw it out." (Pr. 20:5). Once they do catch up ... oh, what joy, what emotion, what understanding it brings. His counsel often starts at a level much deeper than our natural intellect. That's why our love affair starts with "love the Lord with all your heart" and then moves on to "with all your mind". There is a progression present here.

He does this (by-passing our faculties) purposely to avoid areas that can skew the vision He wants us to have. All of us are at different places in our thoughts and emotions, and we therefore interpret whatever we encounter differently. Our Father does not want to be misunderstood! And so He engineered a way of communication that could not be interfered with by our natural faculties.

Bottled at Source

I recently read the label on a bottle of spring water: "Bottled at Source" was printed boldly and proudly on it. The rest of the message emphasised how this water contained no additives or contaminants, but only the natural goodness found at the source, the unpolluted origin. The message was clear: the further from the source, the greater the potential for contamination; the closer to the source, the purer.

This is the same idea Paul had about the message he preached. *"Now I want you to know, brothers, that the gospel preached by me is not based on a human point of view. For I did not receive it from a human source and I was not taught it, but it came by a revelation of Jesus Christ."* Galatians 1:11,12

The first chapter of this letter and much of the second is focused on this concept that no human taught him this message, neither was it the product of his own scholastic efforts. Rather, this message was initiated and communicated by God directly - he received it from the source ... unpolluted, original, authoritative, pure. This gospel is not subject to human interpretation, translation or misrepresentation.

He goes through great lengths to explain that he had no prolonged contact with any of the recognised leaders - in summary: *"But from those recognised as important (what they really were makes no difference to me; God does not show favoritism)—those recognised as important added nothing to me."* (Gal 2:6)

Paul obviously understood the importance of direct, unrestricted contact with the Light of life as opposed to a second-hand religious system that attempts to communicate truth through a man-made hierarchy. Now he undoubtedly thought it important to communicate this message, but the whole purpose of his communication was to introduce the listeners to the Source of these truths and not to set himself up as the source of their spiritual understanding. His attitude is portrayed so clearly in this portion of one of his letters: *"We're not in charge of how you live out the faith, looking over your shoulders, suspiciously critical. We're partners, working alongside you, joyfully expectant. I know that you stand by your own faith, not by ours."* 2 Cor 1:24 MSG

This seems to me a very different approach to that taken by

many religious institutions. Many of these institutions regard themselves, consciously or unconsciously, as the guardians of truth - desiring to control and mediate between their followers and God. In the process these religious systems have become contaminants of the original message, no longer containing the pure message as derived from the source, but mixed with the additives of human tradition and popular interpretation.

No father desires a relationship with his children to be interfered with by a third party broker - speaking to his children via an interpreter. The Father, your Creator, desires a direct, open relationship with you personally. He is confident in the ability He gave you to hear Him and to respond to Him. "*The hearing ear and the seeing eye, The LORD has made them both.*" Pr. 20:12

Jesus, seeing the emptiness of religious festivals and rituals offered a much better alternative. "On the last and most important day of the festival, Jesus stood up and cried out, "*If anyone is thirsty, he should come to Me and drink! The one who believes in Me, as the Scripture has said, will have streams of living water flow from deep within him.*" (John 7:37-38). Jesus has more to offer than religious festivals and rituals; more than external sources of religious experiences. Once you partake of what He has to offer it becomes a source of overflowing life within you.

His way of thinking

Isaiah:55:7,8

Let the wicked one abandon his way,
and the sinful one his thoughts; ….
"For My thoughts are not your thoughts,
and your ways are not My ways."

Notice that having thoughts that are not His thoughts, is described as wicked and sinful - a way of thinking that should be abandoned. God never stated that such a condition is simply human, and therefore we should just accept it. No! He challenges us to forsake such low level thinking. He plainly says that if you don't think like Him, you need to change your thinking!

He desires for you to know His thoughts and His ways. Not only does He desire for you to know His thoughts, but He also wants to teach you how to think as He does. Let's look again at that scripture:

Isaiah:55:7-11
Let the wicked one abandon his way,
and the sinful one his thoughts;
let him return to the LORD,
so He may have compassion on him,
and to our God, for He will freely forgive.
"For My thoughts are not your thoughts,
and your ways are not My ways."

declares the Lord.

"For as heaven is higher than earth,
so My ways are higher than your ways,
and My thoughts than your thoughts.
For just as rain and snow fall from heaven,
and do not return there
without saturating the earth,
and making it germinate and sprout,
and providing seed to sow
and food to eat,
so My word that comes from My mouth
will not return to Me empty,
but it will accomplish what I please,
and will prosper in what I send it to do."

Just like the rain and snow bridge the gap between Heaven and Earth, so His Word bridges the gap between His understanding and ours. He wants to saturate our minds with His thinking; He designed our imagination as fertile soil in which His ideas would germinate and sprout. The fruit of thinking His thoughts, is living His life.

Our Creator desires to be known; our Father wants to be understood, but His desire extends even further. He longs for meaningful companionship with a being that can think on His level; a being that is able to communicate boldly and comfortably in His presence. Such a being exists … it's the one He created in

His own image and likeness … it is you.

Discovering His thoughts has always been a pleasant discovery. He surprises me time and again with His goodness. My best imaginations are always overshadowed by much better realities, when I see things from His perspective. He is better, bigger, wiser, more thorough, more involved, more loving than what we could ever have hoped for. He is exceedingly abundantly above all we could ask or imagine. He invites you right now to come and partake, to boldly come and commune with Him. There are no reasons to hesitate … just let Him surprise you with His goodness.

You,
Time
&
Eternity

One cannot help but be in awe when he contemplates the mysteries of eternity, of life, of the marvelous structure of reality. It is enough if one tries merely to comprehend a little of this mystery every day. Never lose a holy curiosity.

Albert Einstein

Time is often experienced as an inescapable vehicle that carries us from birth to death; a relentless force that propels us from the present to the future. But what is 'time'? We've become so familiar with our measure of time - seconds, hours, days, years - that it is easy to confuse our measures of time with time itself. Our experience of time and our measures of time might be far too narrow because they are limited by our specific point of view.

There are many interesting philosophies about time and even more interesting speculations about what the possibilities might be, if such philosophies were true. I won't explore all these philosophies in depth in this writing - only enough to help us appreciate what the Word has to say about time. For that purpose I'll adopt one of the most basic and helpful definitions of time, namely: a sequence of events.

How we relate to this sequence of events and how God relates to it is very different. Some of the statements in scripture seem at first to contain some grammatical errors, the tenses are all wrong! For instance: *"Before Abraham was, I am"*. In other instances the Word speaks about future events as if they had happened in the past. Hundreds of years before the birth and death of Jesus, Isaiah speaks of His suffering on the cross as a past event: *"...but He was wounded for our transgressions, he was bruised for our iniquities: the chastisement of our peace was upon him, and by his stripes we are healed."* Is 53:5.

I was bemused by an article I read about Tachyons. This is a scientific name for a theoretical particle that travels faster or at the speed of light. The nature of such a particle is truly astounding. For instance, let's imagine one could build a fax machine based on the laws covering tachyons and we call it our tachyons fax machine. If one was to send a fax at 3pm it would arrive at 2pm! The effect precedes the cause. I immediately thought of Mat 8:16-17 in which Jesus heals the sick who were brought to Him. Verse 17 states that this was in fulfilment of what was prophesied by Isaiah. It's again the passage in Isaiah 53 that we looked at earlier. We know that this passage refers to the suffering and death of Christ, but here again the effect (healing) of what He accomplished on the cross is experienced by people long before the cause. Another example of this inversion of time is found in Isaiah 65:24 *"Before they call I answer"*.

These statements draw us into a dimension beyond our normal experience of time. A dimension in which time is a radically different entity from our normal experience of it. The use of the words: *"before Abraham was, I am"* seems to indicate two different dimensions. One in which there is a past, present and future, and one in which there is simply a present. However, it might say more about the nature of God than about the nature of time.

Let's start by looking at the Hebrew understanding of time as found in the Old Testament. We don't find philosophical or abstract debates about the nature of time, as we do in the Greek philosophies of that period. Time is not described as a separate force or an extra dimension, but in rather more concrete terms. Events occurred and these events stood in relation to other events and this was in effect, time. Time has no substance apart from these events. Whereas the Greeks saw time as a separate dimension in which events happened, the Hebrews simply saw events happening and these 'happenings' were time. As such, eternity is never described as timeless, for there could be no events, no experience, no life without time. To be timeless would be lifeless.

The quality of events are given greater significance than the order in which they happened or the duration it took. In some instances events and persons were arranged according to the impact of their occurrence, rather than their chronological sequence. The weightiness and significance of people and events were regarded more important than the exact date of the occurrence. People did things. God did things. Time is the story of these events and has no existence beyond these events.

One of the reasons why eternity is often thought of as timeless is because of our understanding of time. Time is seen as temporal, subject to change, whereas eternity is seen as changeless. However, it is the nature of change that is different in the eternal realm. There is 'change' that decays and there is 'change' that renews. 2 Cor 4:16: *Therefore we do not become discouraged. Though our outer man is [progressively] decaying and wasting away, yet our inner self is being [progressively] renewed day after day.* A blooming flower undergoes change, but every change just further establishes its beauty and essential reality. Proverbs speaks of the life of the righteous being like the rising sun, shining brighter and brighter. The eternal realm does have events and does have change, but every change further confirms the essential reality of this realm and consequently it is not temporal. Eternity is more about absolutes than duration. It's only because of a narrow view of time that we reduced eternity to an endless duration of time - it's so much more! The motion of time can be compared to the motion of a shadow ... eternity is the absolute substance.

Who better to define eternity than Jesus. He said: This is eternal life: that they may know You, the only true God, and the One You have sent - Jesus Christ. Eternal life has much more to do with God, our intimacy with Him, and the quality of life it produces, than it has to do with a long period of time.

There is an event that took place in eternity of such importance and magnitude that it overflowed into our time! This mystery was hidden for ages and generations ... but then it happened: Eternity arrived in time; the infinite filled the finite; the eternal filled the temporal, the unknowable God revealed Himself in a way we can all understand. God became man! His mind was made known; His character unveiled; His opinion of you made clear. Like an ocean emptied into a pond, it filled and changed all time - out of all proportion to the fall of man, is the redemption of man. The Lamb, who was slain from the foundation of the world, was born and walked amongst us.

It is this singular event that gives meaning to all other time. It is only within this one event that all other events can find purpose. This event is God's reference within our time by which all other events are judged. Only within relationship to this event can the temporal, changing, time-bound events find eternal value. Although this single event was concentrated in one individual, Jesus, it included all men. And although it happened before you were born, it has a greater claim on you than your own personal past.

Whether you are aware of it or not, this event affects you ... in fact it is all about you. Paul refers to it as the *fullness of time* (Eph 1:10). He describes it as a singular event that has consequences for all mankind in all ages; an achievement that occurred once and included all without exception. The fullness of time ... so much can be said about it, where does one begin. The fullness of time means:

No time to come can add to what was given in this event; our sense of satisfaction, completeness, fullness has everything to do with appreciating the event that filled all of time, and nothing to do with any future event; we can never exhaust the wealth of understanding and insight that was lavished upon us in this event.

Further on in this letter of Paul, he writes that all of eternity will be a further revelation of the exceeding greatness of God's kindness toward us in this event - in Christ.

Jesus said on a number of occasions: " ...*the time is coming, and now is* ...". He tapped into eternity in such a way that the present contained everything that the future had to offer! After speaking to the Samaritan woman at the well about living water - water that not only satisfies but overflows, He ends off by saying: *"I am he," said Jesus. "You don't have to wait any longer or look any further"*. (John 4:26 MSG). All that eternity has to offer is in Christ and He is present in this very moment.

The Motivation before Creation

The creation of art is not the fulfillment of a need. The world never needed Beethoven's Fifth Symphony until he created it. Now we could not live without it.

Louis Kahn

Original, yet New

Jesus once said: "*My testimony is valid, because I know where I came from and where I'm going.*" (John 8:14). An understanding of our origin and final destiny has a greater influence on our 'now' - our present experience - than anything else.

This great gospel has the most awesome origin and the most triumphant conclusion. In the beginning, before creation, before time as we experience it, before the existence of evil, the God who is love planned to share this love with beings created in His image and likeness. This God, who is all-knowing and able to accomplish all of His purposes, planned a love-affair that would span over eons and conclude with a final victory in which His love conquered all - no contradiction; no evil, for death will die. This gospel is not some new idea, but the ancient, original thought of God. The challenges to our faith and the questions asked of it are not new either, however, we should never allow our answers to become stale. The truth of this message is ever fresh as it finds resonance in us.

John, realising the ancient beginning of this message wrote: "*Dear friends, I am not writing you a new command, but an old command that you have had from the beginning*". But he also realised that this truth remains fresh and current as it finds confirmation in our lives, and so he wrote: "*On the other hand, perhaps it is new, freshly minted as it is in both Christ and you—the darkness on its way out and the True Light already blazing!"*

(1 John 2:7,8)

The Original Motivation

In the beginning was the Word,
and the Word was with God,
and the Word was God.
He was with God in the beginning.
All things were created through Him,
and apart from Him not one thing was created
that has been created. (John 1:1-2)

Imagine what John thought when he began planning this writing. Where does this story begin? Where and when did Christ begin? The Holy Spirit starts to reveal to him a beginning even before the first recorded scripture. Before "*In the beginning God created*" he sees "*In the beginning was the Word, and the Word was with God, and the Word was God*". He sees Christ in God before creation began. He sees Christ before sin entered the world. He sees Christ beyond the context of redemption. He sees Christ as the expression (Word) of God.

Let's imagine this beginning, let's allow the spirit of God to draw us, just like He drew John, to this place in which all things had their origin. Although no science can explain it, although the greatest minds have tried and failed to define it, God is confident that you are able to comprehend the unsearchable; to appreciate the motivation that gave you birth; to remember where you began. In this place there is no space, yet no limit; no creation, yet no emptiness, - there is only God in all His fullness. The one and only true God: a Union of multiple expressions. Within the diversity of this Union there is a free and explosive exchange of that which is most essential to God - love.

You see, although there are many characteristics by which we can describe God, there is only one quality that unifies and harmonises all the other qualities. Much later He inspired a writing that gives us such clear insight into His being:

If I speak the languages of men and of angels, but do not have love, I am a sounding gong or a clanging cymbal. If I have prophecy, and understand all mysteries and all knowledge, and if I have all faith, so that I can move mountains, but do not have love, I am nothing. (1 Cor 13)

These words reveal something about the God of love, namely: It is not His infinite knowledge or intellect, referred to as His omniscience, that is His most essential characteristic. Neither is it His limitless power, known as His omnipotence, that makes Him who He is. Love is at the core of who God is!

Love desires to give ... love is not focused on itself, but desires the benefit of others. Love is not needy, lack-conscious or aware of what it does not have. Love is an expression of abundance; the overflow of joy and satisfaction. Love is not obsessed with its own importance … it does not need the recognition of others. There is no inferiority in love … it is not dependent on affirmation, because love's attention is not on itself but on its target. All God is for man and all He does for man, is out of His own free grace. He does not owe us anything, neither do we have any claim upon this free grace, yet in utter freedom, without any obligation He desires to give it, because that is who He is. His love, His free grace is not some quality or property of His character that can be placed alongside other properties. This is essentially who He is. All other qualities proceed from this central reality: God is love.

In this place; in the beginning; in God, there is no need or lack. It's the abundance and overflow of joy that motivates the 'Logos' - the Logic and Word of God - to calculate and plan a way in which this love would continue to grow and find ever increasing expression throughout all eternity. This God-dream is about a being who has the capacity to receive, to produce and to exchange the same quality of love that flows within God. His plan is not vague or speculative philosophy, but clear and specific … so clear, that He uniquely identifies and names the individuals who would form part of the plan and become part of creation. And so before the foundation of this world, He saw you in Christ. At this point, He made up His mind about you! No matter what detours, no matter what contradictions would come, He determined that you would be His treasure - blameless and innocent before Him in love.

The good news therefore begins, not with any form of human need, but with the free gift of God's grace, which is nothing less than God Himself.

Before it all began

Before His infinite mind, lay infinite possibilities. Within His limitless imagination arose limitless options. God chose from all the possibilities, those which would most accurately express Himself. But in choosing these possibilities, in deciding what to create, there were inevitably some possibilities that were rejected. The possibilities and options that were rejected, later became known as 'evil'. 'Evil' is all the possibilities that are not in harmony with the nature and character of God. Evil is all that He chose not to create. The existence of evil does not mean it has any substance - darkness exists only in the absence of light.

However, the being He imagined to be His companion, would be able to choose 'its' own possibilities. Love, by its very nature, is free. Love can be awakened, encouraged and stirred, but it can never be forced. And so God determined to create man outside of His control! This meant - and He knew it all before - that man would make wrong choices and in doing so create obstacles to ... or maybe opportunities for, the love of God.

How could a completely free and spontaneous being be guaranteed to make the right choices? The 'Logos' calculated uncountable scenarios and configurations of the environment to see if there was a way to guarantee the right choice. The answer was produced after an exceptionally long period of timelessness. The fact that this being would not be all-knowing, yet be imaginative and free, meant that this being would indeed make choices and have preferences other than those chosen by God! This creature would be responsible for choosing 'evil'! For any other logic, this would be an impossible situation - how to plan and purpose the conclusion of this plot, yet give another creature the freedom to choose what role to play within it. But for the Logos, nothing is impossible.

Before anything began, God foresaw the inevitable mistakes, the fall of man, the evil consequences ... but He also saw a way in which to provide for every need, overcome every obstacle and restore man to the glory He intended. And so we read about the grace which was given to us in Christ Jesus before time began! (1 Tim 1:9). Before He created anything, He knew it would cost Him everything to redeem man and fulfil all His purpose ... and so we read about the Lamb that was slain from the foundation of the world. Once again, in His own freedom, He determined to give Himself in His Son, to step out of this eternal unsearchable realm, into the temporal, the realm of fallen man. In giving us grace and truth, He would give nothing less than Himself.

When we realise that our Creator foreknew the whole plot before a single event occurred, we are able to recognise His loving and guiding hand in all things. He knew about the temptations, the choices and the consequences of those choices, long before they happened. *"He declares the end from the beginning"*. Isaiah 46:10 ... He is not the author of all events, but He certainly is wise and able enough to steer even the most evil events toward the conclusion that He pre-ordained.

I'm so glad God is not nervous or anxious about the life He imagined for us. He is resting in the full assurance of who we really are and who He really is. He invites us to join Him in that same rest; to see things from His perspective. Realise that there is no obstacle He cannot overcome; there is no problem that surprises Him - before you ask, He has answered.

The Journey Begins

When I consider Your heavens, the work of Your fingers,
The moon and the stars, which You have ordained;
What is man that You take thought of him,
And the son of man that You care for him?

Psalm 8:3-4

The 'time' of planning came to an end and the time for action began. Creation was spoken into existence. The colours, the dimensions of space, the sound that sustains the atom, the energy that sustains each element, burst forth from the imagination of God into ... something that has never been before ... a dimension separate from Him, yet intimately upheld by Him. No expense was spared, no space was too vast, no speed was too fast, no detail was too small, when He prepared the environment in which the masterpiece of His imagination - man - would live and move and grow into all that He imagined us to be.

When man opened his eyes for the first time, all was ready, all was prepared. The first words man heard were words that established them as the rulers of this world, and the objects of God's approval ... "*God saw all that He had made, and it was very good.*" (Gen 1:28) All these blessings were given not because of anything man did to deserve it or earn it, but simply because man was designed and created for this purpose. No other creature had the spirit capacity for companionship with God. No other spirit being was given the unique position of stewardship over creation. Man was uniquely positioned in both the spirit realm and the physical realm. And this position was not something man achieved, but had simply received. It is also important to understand that God did not owe man anything - the blessings He gave were out of His own free desire to do so. Never was 'obligation' any part of the relationship God imagined. As long as man remained in right relationship with the Creator, he would also remain in right relationship with creation.

God had more in mind than a wonderful garden and occasional visits with man and so step by step He began to lead man into a deeper appreciation of His purpose. Adam was given the task of naming all the creatures. In the process of doing this, it became obvious that all these creatures had companions ... but none were compatible with man: "*...no helper was found who was like him.*" Intimacy is linked to recognising likeness.

Isn't it just so thoughtful of God, that instead of simply telling man that it is not good to be alone, He prepares a task, an experience in which man comes to this conclusion. He is not interested in simply enforcing His thoughts on you, He wants you to use the imagination and intellect He has given you to come to the same conclusions as Him. (Gen 2:15-20). By leading man into this experience, our Creator reveals something of His own desire and motivation. He too desired a companion in whom He would recognise His own likeness.

"*So the LORD God caused a deep sleep to come over the man, and he slept. God took one of his ribs and closed the flesh at that place. Then the LORD God made the rib He had taken from the man into a woman and brought her to the man. And the man said:*

This one, at last, is bone of my bone,
and flesh of my flesh;

this one will be called woman,

for she was taken from man." Gen 2:21-23

Many eons later, another man would be 'put to sleep', his side would be split open and a new creation would be formed. *"... Who has heard of such a thing? Who has seen such things? Shall a land be born in one day? Or shall a nation be brought forth in a moment? ..."* (Is 66:8 AMP) In speaking about the relationship between a husband and wife, Paul adds this: *"This mystery is profound, but I am talking about Christ and the church."* (Eph 5:32) In another letter He writes: *"... we speak God's hidden wisdom in a mystery, which God predestined before the ages for our glory."* Part of the mystery of our likeness to God, is demonstrated in this diversity, yet union of Adam and Eve. She is bone of his bone and flesh of his flesh, she is like him, came from within him, yet is separate. The secret of their union, yet distinctiveness, mirrors the secret of our relationship with God.

So each of these journeys or experiences that He led man into, weren't isolated events - they were all part of a much bigger picture. Through each of these events God was revealing more and more of Himself to man, and man was entering deeper and deeper into an intimate understanding of God. Adam and Eve were all God imaged them to be in the sense that a seed contains all that is required to produce a tree, but they did not yet blossom into all God foresaw for them.

However, this process was interrupted. Not everything God purposed for man was fulfilled in Eden. For instance there was a tree of life of which man had never partaken. Despite an explicit warning, Adam chose to ignore God's instruction and listen to another. Next, I want us to look at some of the consequences of this disobedience. It is however important to recognise that Adam's act of disobedience cannot be fully understood in isolation. Adam stands in relation to Christ like a shadow - it is only in the light of Christ that this shadow finds its true form.

When man stepped out of his position and relationship with God, all of creation stepped out of relationship with man. Creation responded to man the way man responded to God. The ground that willingly and spontaneously produced food for man's sustenance, would now only yield what was earned through the sweat of his brow. Adam and Eve suddenly had to deal with issues such as dependence and dominance. Man entered a new order, known as the kingdom of darkness; the reign of death. This new government was not located outside of man, but a government that's described as a *"...law at work in the members of my body, waging war against the law of my mind and making me a prisoner"*.

But what remained the same? One of the words often used to describe this condition of man, is the word 'lost'. Man was no longer in the possession of his owner. However, there is a beautiful promise hidden in this word, for if something is 'lost' it also implies that it belongs! A thief never becomes the rightful owner of what is stolen. The kingdom of darkness never became our natural home - it is always a kingdom in which we are lost, we never belong. The problem is that the longer one lingers in a foreign land, the less one remembers of where you came from and with time, the foreign becomes familiar. At the head of this dark kingdom resides the father of lies. All he ever gave birth to are lies - the rest of what he controls is stolen property. No matter how comfortable and familiar the stolen property becomes in his kingdom - he will never be their Creator, never their rightful owner. Although the father of lies took possession of all that was given to Adam, the rightful owner was still the Lord of heaven and earth for "*the earth is the Lord's, and all its fullness, the world and those who dwell therein.*"

Jesus once spoke about a lost coin and the determination of the owner to find it. The lost coin never lost its value ... and the owner knows this. Although man began to forget his origin, our Maker never forgot His own. He always knew our value, despite our location or condition. Part of His plan to rescue us from the kingdom of darkness, was to remind us, to bring us back into a consciousness of our beginning in Him. From a human point of view, "*... you forget the LORD your Maker, Who stretched out the heavens And laid the foundations of the earth*", but from God's point of view, "*...can a woman forget her nursing child, And not have compassion on the son of her womb? Surely they may forget,*

"...All the ends of the world
Shall remember and turn to the LORD,
And all the families of the nations
Shall worship before You.
For the kingdom is the LORD's,
And He rules over the nations." Psalms 22:27-28

Another term that is used to describe this state of man, is 'sick'. Any physician knows the difference between the patient and the sickness. The sickness is a foreign influence that needs to be destroyed. One does not treat the patient like the sickness, neither does one treat the sickness as if it is the patient. When the foreign influence is destroyed the patient can once again be himself or herself. I've heard people talk about the sinfulness of man as if it is the very quality that defines man. It is not! There is a cure. Long before the fall of man God defined man as His own likeness and His own image, and in the fullness of time He affirmed our identity when the Word became flesh. When the Word became a man, it also became the Word about man and man is nothing more and nothing less than what this Word declares him to be.

We should always remember that in this tragedy, man was not simply the victim, but an active participant and chose his own fate. Man endangered himself and continues to endanger himself. Man abandoned the authority, the dominion and the stewardship that was given to him and in so doing, gave a perfect opportunity for the thief to steal. In short, man was not an innocent victim, he was guilty. To say it another way: if there was an insurance company that covered Adam and Eve in the event of a loss - their policy would not pay out because of their negligence. They were partly responsible for the situation. There was actual and real guilt both on the side of man and obviously on the side of the thief.

The master plan therefore included both the necessary reminder and revelation to loose man from the grip of darkness, but also an actual price that had to be paid for the legitimate guilt.

The Crescendo

He is the image of the invisible God, the firstborn over all creation. For by him all things were created: things in heaven and on earth, visible and invisible, whether thrones or powers or rulers or authorities; all things were created by him and for him. ... so that in everything he might have the supremacy. For God was pleased to have all his fullness dwell in him, and through him to reconcile to himself all things, whether things on earth or things in heaven, by making peace through his blood, shed on the cross.

Collosians 1:15-20

Throughout ancient times God spoke in many fragments and glimpses of prophetic thought to our fathers. Now, the sum total of His conversation with man has finally culminated in a son; He is the official heir of all things, He is after all the author of the ages. In Him everything finds their destiny. (Christ is the crescendo of God's conversation with us.) He makes the glory (intent) of God visible in radiant reflection, He gives stature to the character and person of God. (Gen.1:26,27.)This final powerful utterance of God (the incarnation) is the vehicle that carries the weight of the universe. The content of His message celebrates the fact that God took it upon Himself to successfully purge and acquit mankind. Jesus is now His right hand of power, seated in the boundless measure of His majesty. He occupies the highest seat of authority.

Heb. 1:1-3 Mirror Translation

All the prophets bore witness and pointed towards an event; a person, in which the mystery - the fullness of God's purpose - would be made known. It was not because of a lack of diligence that they only saw and spoke in fragments and glimpses, but because of the enormity of this revelation. There was only One who was worthy to open the seals; only One who would have the strength and wisdom to accurately reflect God's original idea; only One who witnessed and was part of God's original motivation to create. The prophets saw glimpses of the mind of God, but Jesus is the mind of God.

In no way does this belittle the prophets, but rather it

emphasises the significance of Christ. The messages that came through the prophets had such rich variety, they were relevant in so many different generations and were communicated in such a diversity of ways, but they were all moving towards a climax - the crescendo of God's conversation with man. The prophets spoke, wrote and sometimes used dramatic action to communicate their message - Jesus is the message. The prophets often spoke a word that was relevant for their generation, their time and situation - Jesus is the complete and eternal Word, always relevant, always fresh. The prophets bore witness to the reality and truth they saw - Jesus is that reality, is that truth. He is the very brilliance and light of God's character and His aim is not simply to reveal truth to us, but to make us true. As we behold Him we are transformed into that same image!

The One who began it all, the Author of the ages, has not forsaken what He made. He is as surely the Lord of 'destiny' as He is the Lord of creation. The Creator is also the Redeemer. He has not retreated into being a distant observer, a purely transcendent God, but continues to be intimately involved, sustaining all existence, upholding the universe.

When John speaks about the Word that became flesh, He is saying that the very mind of God, the reason and very life of God was made visible, so that we no longer have to grope in the darkness, but know His thoughts towards us. He is the true or real light - the essence and reality of everything. If you want to know what God is like, look at what Jesus is like. Jesus said "I am the Way, the Truth, and the Life". In this one statement He identifies Himself as the ultimate reality, the mind of God revealed.

God's Word is Jesus Christ. There is only one Word and only one mediator between man and God, the man Christ Jesus. All He has to say to us, He said in Christ. All He has to give to us, He gave in Jesus Christ, for in Christ, He gave Himself in all His fullness. Not only did He become man, but in His free gift of grace, He makes us like Himself. Our entire relation with God, happens within this Word. This is the Word that planned our existence, this is the Word through whom we were created, this is the Word that is our mediation, this is the Word that reveals the secret of our identity and the purpose of our existence, and this Word is our only hope and destiny.

The Word Eternal

Long before the first line of scripture
was penned on papyrus scroll,
the Word, unwritten,
existed as the mind of God.

Before the books were gathered
collated as sacred text,
the Word, intangible; invisible,

was planning, was ordering
the ages that were to come.
This Word predates the Bible,
this Word predates creation,
this Word is alive and active
and speaking still today.

"Heaven is my throne room;
I rest my feet on earth.
So what kind of house
will you build me?" says God.

What kind of doctrine could enfold Him,
What kind of information could define Him,
What kind of book could contain Him?

Yet, despite His boundless nature,
within His infinite wisdom,
He devised a crafty plan, by which
His thoughts, His intents
would fit themselves into
the form of a humble seed:
The DNA of His own life,
encrypted within the written Word.

And so began the writing
of that which we now call:

the Bible - the Scriptures.
Within the limitations; imperfections
of human words and human authors
God placed His eternal perfect seed.

A seed is not a tree;
the Scriptures are not our God,
Yet a seed is the beginning, the start -
provided with fruitful soil,
encouraged by water and light,
a seed gives birth to a being
much greater than itself.

His plan foresaw the day
in which this seed would blossom
no longer encrypted; no longer disguised
but fully expressed in the person
of Jesus - the Christ - the Son
The One who was in the beginning
revealed within our midst
Immanuel - God with us -
the Word became flesh.

His desire is still the same:
for His Word to break free of the boundaries
of letters and text and theories
and yet again, become flesh,

and yet again find expression in a person:

you - the chosen - the offspring of God.

So as we approach the Scriptures,

do more than read what is written -

listen to what is spoken.

So once again we can encounter

the mind, the voice, the person

who spoke long before

pen or paper was born.

(by Andre Rabe)

This Great Salvation

Concerning this salvation, the prophets who prophesied about the grace that would come to you searched and carefully investigated. They inquired into what time or what circumstances the Spirit of Christ within them was indicating when He testified in advance to the messianic sufferings and the glories that would follow. It was revealed to them that they were not serving themselves but you concerning things that have now been announced to you through those who preached the gospel to you by the Holy Spirit sent from heaven. 1 Pet 1:10-12

When they inquired about the time to which all their writings pointed, the event that would be the fulfilment of God's purpose and the release of His glory on earth, the Spirit of God within them pointed towards the sufferings of Christ. They realised that we (those who came after the suffering of Christ) would be the beneficiaries of this event. How many continue to search the scriptures, trying to find another prophesy that points to another time or event, and in the process neglect the greatest event - this great salvation.

The Jews divided time into two parts, namely: the present age, and the age to come. The 'present age' was subject to evil and the 'age to come' would be the perfect age in which God rules. In between these two ages they saw the 'Day of the Lord' which was, as it were the birth pangs of the new age. The writer of Hebrews is saying that the age of glimpses, fragments is gone and the age of completeness has come. The time of shadows and grasping in the dark has gone, the time of reality and truth has come. In Jesus "... *the darkness is passing away, and the true light is already shining*" and "*you will do well to heed this word as a light that shines in a dark place, until the day dawns and the morning star rises in your hearts.*" (1John2:8, 2 Pet 1:19). Jesus is not just another messenger of 'the present age', but He is the Day of the Lord, giving birth to a whole new dispensation.

God anticipated a time and a person in which He would reveal Himself in such clarity and completeness, that for all eternity it would be known as the crescendo, the sum total of His conversation with man. Just as He spoke creation into existence, this declaration would once again be a word of such magnitude that it would give birth to a whole new creation. Just as He originally said: "*let light shine out of darkness*", He would once again speak a word that would shine with the knowledge of the favour of God; a message that would radiate the character of God with such accuracy that it would dispel all darkness, destroy all ignorance of His love and leave man without excuse to remain distant. This event would mark the end of the old Adamic race, a race defined by the fall of man, and be the birth of a new humanity, a humanity which God reconciled to Himself, not holding their trespassed against them, a humanity defined by Christ - His final Word regarding man.

Identity revealed

In the face of Christ Jesus the eternal purpose of God, His original intent and thoughts towards man were made plain. This revelation destroys every false identity and unlocks the truth about us. The light that confronted Saul on the way to Damascus was both a destructive force and a life-giving encounter. The flaming fire of the presence of God eternally destroyed Saul, and simultaneously brought forth Paul - the true person that God had in mind since the beginning. As Paul continued to look into this light, he saw the face of Christ shining with the knowledge of the glory of God. As he looked deeply, he became aware of the real significance of Christ, a significance far beyond the miracles He performed, a significance far beyond the few years He spent on earth. He began to recognise, in the face of Christ, the true identity of mankind.

It is this insight into Christ which takes us beyond a mere historic appreciation of Him, into a present awareness of the One who lives; the One who represents my innocence at the right hand of God.

Jesus once asked: "Who do men say that I am?". After His disciples gave Him all the current opinions and hearsay stories, He asked: "And you, who do you say that I am?". There is an appointed time for you to move beyond popular opinion and come to your own conclusion. Can you hear Him asking you that question today: "Who do you say that I am?" Seeing Him for who He truly is, is not an intellectual exercise; it's not simply reading about what He did or said. Even His disciples who were with Him did not come to an accurate conclusion about Him from observing Him in the natural. It was only when the Father revealed His own point of view to Peter, that Peter started to appreciate the real Christ. Jesus then immediately started speaking to Peter about his true identity - that He was a piece of a rock carved and originating in another rock. Reminds us of Is 51: "*You who seek the LORD: Look to the rock from which you were hewn*" In realising His true identity, you discover your own. "*The only accurate way to understand ourselves is by what God is and by what he does for us, not by what we are and what we do for him.*" (Rom 12:3 MSG).

But we all, with unveiled face, beholding as in a mirror the glory of the Lord, are being transformed into the same image from glory to glory. (2 Cor 3:18 NAS). Jesus Christ, the Word made flesh, is the reflection of God's original thought about us, the means by which we were created, the mediator through whom we are justified and made blameless, the mirror in whom we see the truth that we were indeed created in His image and likeness.

Christ is the revelation of your true identity. "*When Christ, who is our life, is revealed, then you also will be revealed with Him in glory.*" (Col 3:4 NAS) The word 'when' in the Greek is in the present continuous tense. In other words 'whenever' is probably a better translation. The Mirror translation says it this way: "*Every time Christ is revealed as our life, we are being co-revealed in the same glory (likeness and image of God) being united together with Him.*"

One
Man's
Achievement

"God is righteous. He is not mocked. What man sows he must also reap. But God has taken it upon Himself to reap this fatal harvest. In man's own place and on man's behalf, God has sown new seed. God has placed Himself under the accusation and condemnation which stand over godless Adam. And God Himself, in their place and ours, became for us the true man from whose way we have strayed. God has thereby spoken. His word of forgiveness, His word of the new commandment, of reserrection of the flesh and an eternal life."

Karl Barth

Through many ages man tried and failed to raise himself out of the state he was in. Although there were moments of greatness, glimpses of freedom, there was no permanent victory over the law of sin and death that operated in man. Good deeds and noble thoughts were constantly contradicted by the evil and depravity that was never far away. Even the most sincere religious endeavours failed to release man from the battle raging within him. For those who sincerely sought after righteousness, the realisation came slowly but surely: we can do nothing to save ourselves; we are completely helpless.

In God's long range plan, there is a movement from fall to grace, from darkness to light, from death to life, from condemnation to justification, from bondage to liberty, from identification with Adam to identification with Christ. This movement has only one conclusion, only one destination. We saw in the previous chapter how this new day began in the fullness of time in the event of Jesus Christ.

Adam represents man's choice to exist in a lesser reality ... a non-reality compared to that for which he was designed. Man, as identified in Adam, does not live in the freedom he was made for; he does not enjoy the relationship with God or man that he could. This however is not man's destiny. In the death of Christ, God judges and condemns this existence, reveals it for the nothingness it is and as such dooms it to pass away.

In the death and resurrection of Jesus Christ, He proclaims and achieves the final end of the old and the endless reality of the new. His death is both the judgement and condemnation of the old man, the man as identified in fallen Adam, as well as the vindication of the new man, the victory of grace. In this achievement He reveals that His grace ultimately prospers, His love never fails, His purpose cannot be withheld. Although man, as identified in Adam, stands guilty sinful and condemned, His word is indeed one of forgiveness, release and justification. In Christ, His final word about man and the only word that will endure, man stands blameless, innocent and accepted.

Romans 5:12-21 (AMP)

Therefore, as sin came into the world through one man, and death as the result of sin, so death spread to all men, [no one being able to stop it or to escape its power] because all men sinned.

[To be sure] sin was in the world before ever the Law was given, but sin is not charged to men's account where there is no law [to transgress].

Yet death held sway from Adam to Moses [the Lawgiver], even over those who did not themselves transgress [a positive command] as Adam did. Adam was a type (prefigure) of the One Who was to come [in reverse, the former destructive, the Latter saving].

But God's free gift is not at all to be compared to the trespass [His grace is out of all proportion to the fall of man]. For if many died through one man's falling away (his lapse, his offense), much more profusely did God's grace and the free gift [that comes] through the undeserved favor of the one Man Jesus Christ abound and overflow to and for [the benefit of] many.

Nor is the free gift at all to be compared to the effect of that one [man's] sin. For the sentence [following the trespass] of one [man] brought condemnation, whereas the free gift [following] many transgressions brings justification (an act of righteousness).

For if because of one man's trespass (lapse, offense) death reigned through that one, much more surely will those who receive [God's] overflowing grace (unmerited favor) and the free gift of righteousness [putting them into right standing with Himself] reign as kings in life through the one Man Jesus Christ (the Messiah, the Anointed One).

Well then, as one man's trespass [one man's false step and falling away led] to condemnation for all men, so one Man's act of righteousness [leads] to acquittal and right standing with God and life for all men.

For just as by one man's disobedience (failing to hear, heedlessness, and carelessness) the many were constituted sinners, so by one Man's obedience the many will be constituted righteous (made acceptable to God, brought into right standing with Him).

But then Law came in, [only] to expand and increase the trespass [making it more apparent and exciting opposition]. But where sin increased and abounded, grace (God's unmerited favor) has surpassed it and increased the more and superabounded,

So that, [just] as sin has reigned in death, [so] grace (His unearned and undeserved favor) might reign also through righteousness (right standing with God) which issues in eternal life through Jesus Christ (the Messiah, the Anointed One) our Lord.

Adam missed the mark and opened the door for death to reign. The death he speaks of here is not merely physical death, although that is part of it. Adam cut himself off from the source of life - life that awakened expression and exuberance in man. Instead he allowed the government of death to take control. Death suppresses; death silences; death dominates, manipulates and controls. This spiritual death spread to all men.

Under this government, everyone gets exactly what they deserve ... the wages of sin is death. And ignorance is no excuse! If you have a deadly disease, it does not matter whether you know it or not, it will still kill you. That is exactly what happened before the Law was given. Even though men sinned in ignorance, they were still under the sway of death.

So Adam and Christ are alike in the sense that what they did affected all men, whether men knew it or not. But that is as far as the comparison can go. What they achieved and what they represent is in fact incomparable. It is not equal parts of one whole, it is out of all proportion. The effect of Adam's fall is doomed to pass away. The last Adam - Christ - pronounced final judgement on that state of affairs and simultaneously introduced a new creation, a new kingdom and "*...of the increase of His government and peace there will be no end*".

Adam's one offence meant that the whole mass of humanity deserved death. God's gift however is not based on what is deserved; it is not based on men repeating his deed of righteousness, the way men repeated deeds of sin. No this free gift has nothing to do with anything man does or does not do. It overflows out of the superabundance of God's own gracious character. *"For out of His fullness we have all received one grace after another and spiritual blessing upon spiritual blessing and even favor upon favor and gift heaped upon gift. For while the Law was given through Moses, grace and truth came through Jesus Christ"*. *"Who was put to death because of our misdeeds and was raised because of our justification"*. the Amplified adds the following: *"making our account balance and absolving us from all guilt before God."* (John 1:16, Rom 4:25)

The effect of their deeds is also incomparable in that one sin resulted in condemnation for everyone. Yet after many transgressions, which logically would mean even greater condemnation for everyone, Christ achieves a feat which results in everyone being proclaimed righteous!

The government of death enforced itself on all who came after Adam yet its influence is destined to pass away. The overflowing grace of God does not enforce itself on anyone, but persistently presents itself to be received. It never loses hope, it believes the best, for it knows the truth about man. In receiving this gift we take back the dominion that death had over us, the dominion that rightfully belongs to us, and reign as kings in life through the one man, Jesus Christ.

Christ established a new order, a new creation. Although it is not fully visible yet, is has been fully accomplished and as such is fully available to each of us. It is a new order, but also the original order - the order in which we stand in a unique relationship with God and a unique relationship with creation. The potential that Adam never achieved, the heights of intimacy he never fully knew, the depth of connection that he only started to appreciate, was demonstrated and achieved in Christ. He is the measure of the perfect man - man as God sees him.

The
Secret of
Contentment

*To walk in the light as He is in the light means to see your life
and everything that concerns you, exclusively from your Father's
point of view. You are indeed the focus of your Father's favour. To
be convinced of your origin in God and the fact that God rescued
His image and likeness in you in Christ is the vital energy of the
law of liberty. To reflect the opinion of God gives you radiance that
makes your life irresistibly attractive.*

Francois Du Toit

The introduction to this book focuses on man's search for contentment. Paul, in the midst of dire circumstances wrote: "*I have learnt the secret of contentment, whatever my circumstances.*" and "*As you read you will understand my insight into the mystery of Christ.*" (Phil 4:11 & Eph. 3:4)

The secret to our contentment lies in discovering that which satisfies God. We can only be satisfied with that which satisfies Him! He designed us in such a way that nothing short of that which gives Him contentment, will give us contentment. Lets look at what satisfies God.

Gen 2:1-2: *Thus the heavens and the earth were finished, and all the host of them. And on the seventh day God ended His work which He had done; and He rested on the seventh day from all His work which He had done.*

Why did God rest on the seventh day? Was it because He was tired or weary after all that work? Did He simply need a break? Can't be, because Isaiah 40:28 says:

Do you not know?
Have you not heard?
Yahweh is the everlasting God,
the Creator of the whole earth.
He never grows faint or weary;
there is no limit to His understanding.

So, if God never gets tired, never needs a break, then why did He enter His rest? Another interesting point about the seventh day, the day of rest, is that unlike the other days, it has no evening ... no end. It is an eternal day.

The answer to why He rests becomes clearer if we look at the end of day six. Gen 1:31: "*And God saw everything that He had made, and behold, it was very good (suitable, pleasant) and He approved it completely. He rested on the seventh day from all His work*". The word translated 'from' can also be translated 'because off'. He was satisfied with what He made, His workmanship. It was the completeness of His creation, the fact that it was very good, that filled and fills Him with contentment. After each day of creation He declared that it was good, but after making man, He declared that it was very good!

Gen 1:28: "*And God blessed them...*" The word 'blessed' (baw-rak) is defined as an act of adoration such as kneeling.

Man's first experience was the overwhelming display of God's favour and adoration! The desire within man to worship God was birthed by this experience of God's adoration – the only appropriate response is to reflect back the adoration He gives. Man alone can appreciate and respond to His love on this level.

I remember that as a young boy of about 15, I desperately sought to please God. I constantly scrutinised my life for things

I thought had to change to make me more attractive to God. One afternoon, lying on my bed, I again began evaluating my behaviour, searching for ways to eliminate what might be offensive. Suddenly, I became aware of God smiling over me. His favour overwhelmed me. It had nothing to do with how I performed, He just adored me because He wanted to. I realised that it was not my behaviour that attracted His favour, it was who I am. He adores what He made.

The realisation of His favour, independent of my behaviour, is what enables me to spontaneously do what pleases Him. It became blatantly obvious how ridiculous it is to try and earn His favour. His approval is out of all proportion to your best achievement. It is bigger than the best deed could ever deserve. It can only be received as a gift.

The invitation to enter the rest of God remains.
Heb 4:1-10 (AMP)

Therefore, while the promise of entering His rest still holds and is offered [today], let us be afraid [to distrust it], lest any of you should think he has come too late and has come short of [reaching] it.

For indeed we have had the glad tidings proclaimed to us just as truly as they [the Israelites of old did when the good news of deliverance from bondage came to them]; but the message they heard did not benefit them, because it was not mixed with faith by those who heard it; neither were they united in faith with the ones [Joshua and Caleb] who heard (did believe).

For we who have believed do enter that rest, in accordance with His declaration that those [who did not believe] should not enter when He said, As I swore in My wrath, They shall not enter My rest; and this He said although [His] works had been completed and prepared [and waiting for all who would believe] from the foundation of the world.

For in a certain place He has said this about the seventh day: And God rested on the seventh day from all His works.

And [they forfeited their part in it, for] in this [passage] He said, They shall not enter My rest.

Seeing then that the promise remains over [from past times] for some to enter that rest, and that those who formerly were given the good news about it and the opportunity, failed to appropriate it and did not enter because of disobedience,

Again He sets a definite day, Today, [and gives another opportunity of securing that rest] saying through David after so long a time in the words already quoted, Today, if you would hear His voice and when you hear it, do not harden your hearts.

[This mention of a rest was not a reference to their entering into Canaan.] For if Joshua had given them rest, He [God] would not speak afterward about another day.

So then, there is still awaiting a full and complete Sabbath-rest reserved for the people of God;

For he who has once entered [God's] rest also has ceased from human labors, just as God rested from those labors peculiarly His *own.*

Let us therefore be zealous and exert ourselves and strive diligently to enter that rest [of God, to know and experience it for ourselves], that no one may fall or perish by the same kind of unbelief and disobedience.

The writer of Hebrews starts this passage with such a clear instruction: Do not disqualify yourself! Don't think it's too late or you have somehow come short of reaching this place of contentment.

So many have given up on searching for contentment, and simply settled into a routine of survival. Life is so much more than routine, so much more than survival - there is a place of contentment and it is within your reach. The only obstacle, the only enemy you should fear, is your own judgement, your own arguments that would disqualify you from this rest.

One of the pictures the writer of Hebrews uses to illustrate this, is the event in which the Israelites were on the brink of entering the promised land which God gave them. Yet they judged themselves inferior, too weak to take it. They missed the opportunity, not because God withheld it from them, but because their own perspective of themselves was skewed. They chose to believe that it was simply too good to be true. God's invitation remains the same ... don't make the same mistake as those who considered themselves disqualified.

"*but the message they heard did not benefit them, because it was not mixed with faith*". There is a reaction that takes place when you mix faith with hearing this message. The product of this reaction is: benefit. It's important to realise that truth remains true whether you believe it or not. '*for we can do nothing against the truth, but only for the truth*' (2 Cor 13:8)

But there is something greater than adoring the truth from a distance ... looking at the promised land from the desert. There is great benefit in embracing this truth and allowing it to embrace you.

The key is in how we hear. There are many ways of hearing. There is casual hearing, suspicious hearing, occasional hearing. However the benefit of these truths are only released when we 'fix our attention'. Heb 3:1 encourages us to 'consider' or 'fix our attention' on Jesus. This is not a casual glance. This is looking deeply, in such a way that the true meaning becomes visible.

We often think of obedience or disobedience in terms of actions. But actions are simply the symptoms. It begins with how we hear. In fact the root meaning of the word 'obey' means 'to hear'. Jesus also spoke about our hearing and said: "*Therefore take heed how you hear. For whoever has, to him more will be given; and whoever does not have, even what he seems to have will be taken from him*". Again it is obvious that how we hear will either enrich or impoverish us.

Heb 5:11-12

Concerning this we have much to say which is hard to explain, since you have become dull in your hearing and sluggish even slothful in spiritual insight. For even though by this time you ought to be teaching others, you actually need someone to teach you over again the very first principles of God's Word.

Dullness of hearing will postpone the rest, the contentment God has prepared for you. Sharpness of hearing will cancel time and distance and release the benefit of this great gospel. The secret of contentment is seeing what God sees, seeing from His point of view and coming to the conclusion that what He made is complete - nothing can be added or taken away. His workmanship is indeed very good.

Living out of Fullness

Everything of God gets expressed in him, so you can see and hear him clearly. You don't need a telescope, a microscope, or a horoscope to realize the fullness of Christ, and the emptiness of the universe without him. When you come to him, that fullness comes together for you, too. His power extends over everything. Entering into this fullness is not something you figure out or achieve. It's not a matter of being circumcised or keeping a long list of laws. No, you're already in—insiders—not through some secretive initiation rite but rather through what Christ has already gone through for you

Collosians 2:9-11 (MSG)

Contentment is not just a theoretical concept, but the place from which you can practically live. In this chapter we'll explore the very real implications of entering, abiding and living out of this position of fullness.

Col 2:11 – *Entering into this fullness is not something you figure out or achieve.* ....and then Gal 3:19-21 *What actually took place is this: I tried keeping rules and working my head off to please God, and it didn't work. So I quit being a "law man" so that I could be God's man. Christ's life showed me how, and enabled me to do it. I identified myself completely with him. Indeed, I have been crucified with Christ. My ego is no longer central. It is no longer important that I appear righteous before you or have your good opinion, and I am no longer driven to impress God. Christ lives in me. The life you see me living is not "mine," but it is lived by faith in the Son of God, who loved me and gave himself for me. I am not going to go back on that.*

Paul found a greater motivation than being driven to impress God! That motivation is the realisation that God is already impressed with you!

I am convinced that our experience of His fullness, our grasp of the love that surpasses knowledge has everything to do with simply being aware of what He achieved on our behalf. Fruit is not an effort for a fruit tree – it is the natural and spontaneous product that occurs when the life within the tree is too abundant for simple survival – it has to overflow into fruit. Draw upon the reality of His indwelling – there is more in you than what you know.

There is a 'place' where we experience the peace, the fountain of life. The question is how do we 'abide' in this place, rather than visit it from time to time.

Rom 6:6-11 (AMP)

We know that our old self was nailed to the cross with Him in order that [our] body [which is the instrument] of sin might be made ineffective and inactive for evil, that we might no longer be the slaves of sin.

For when a man dies, he is freed (loosed, delivered) from [the power of] sin.

Now if we have died with Christ, we believe that we shall also live with Him, because we know that Christ, being once raised from the dead, will never die again; death no longer has power over Him.

For by the death He died, He died to sin [ending His relation to it] once for all; and the life that He lives, He is living to God [in unbroken fellowship with Him].Even so consider yourselves also dead to sin and your relation to it broken, but alive to God [living in unbroken fellowship with Him] in Christ Jesus.

I'm exited about that phrase: 'living in unbroken fellowship with Him'. So much of the religious teachings I have heard were about 'dying to sin/old self' … whatever they called it, it came down to some sort of effort from my side to achieve or reach this place of fellowship. What strikes me in these verses is that the death we died to sin is a singular event – 'once and for all'! It is not supposed to be a continual struggle. And the way I finally put to death the old man is by: 'considering, calculating, coming to this conclusion': I died with Him! …. I was also raised with Him to a new life. My life is now consumed by new realities. I no longer live to attain anything, but because of what He attained on my behalf. The throne room of God is not our final destination, it is our current position. We were raised with Him, and seated with Him in heavenly places, from there to reign and rule in life through Jesus Christ.

I am convinced that the 'old man' – the flesh – thrives off whatever attention we give it. It shrivels to its appointed place of insignificance when we place all our attention on Christ – who He is and who we are because of who He is.

Psalms 17:15 *As for me, I will behold thy face in righteousness: I shall be satisfied, when I awake, in thy likeness.*

To 'wake up' requires no conscious effort – it is simply the point at which my mind's attention shifts from unreal imaginations to seeing reality.

Desire

Even our desires can be birthed out of this place of fullness, rather than a consciousness of lack. What is the first thing that comes to mind when you hear the word 'desire'. If you were brought up religiously, chances are that you associate desire with something evil, something to be avoided. Religion has made much of the negative side of desire, how evil and destructive it can be. The Bible, however, has many positive and exciting things to say about desire.

To celebrate our eighteenth wedding anniversary, Mary-Anne and I spent a long weekend in the Lake District. The first evening we found a restaurant that was highly recommended. I ordered scallops for a starter - something I've only eaten once before and thoroughly enjoyed. The scallops weren't that good this time, but the rest of the meal was excellent.

Twenty four hours later both of us became desperately ill. We later discovered that scallops are able to eat a certain algae that is highly poisonous to people. I lost my appetite completely (very unusual). I had no desire for anything. I did not want to read. I did not even want to think!

Two days later when we started to recover, I thought of the Buddhist concept called 'Nirvana' which means a total absence of all desire. After experiencing a fraction of what it means to be without any desire, I could not understand why anyone would aspire to reach such a place! For me it was the closest thing to death while still breathing. I later learnt that 'Nirvana' is exactly that: annihilation.

There is no fulfilment, no satisfaction, no contentment, without desire. Proverbs 13:12 says that a desire fulfilled is a tree of life.

Psalms 20:4: "*May He grant you according to your heart's desire and fulfill all your plans.*"

Jesus taught about desire as well. John 15:7: "*If you live in Me [abide vitally united to Me] and My words remain in you and continue to live in your hearts, ask whatever you will, and it shall be done for you.*"

To abide means to remain, to make your home in, as apposed to an occasional visit. In Mark 4 Jesus speaks about soil that is hardened, soil in which the seed cannot remain or abide, because the birds eat it before it finds root. When Jesus explains this parable from verse eighteen onward He shows that the soil symbolises our understanding, our imagination. Mark 4:20: "*And those sown on the good soil are the ones who hear the Word and receive and accept and welcome it and bear fruit--some thirty times as much as was sown, some sixty times as much, and some a hundred times as much.*"

Allow His word to find its permanent home within your

imagination. Embrace His thoughts, welcome them and watch as the fruit-bearing effect of the seed of God's word, God's logic, finds expression in the environment that He designed as the natural habitation of the Logos - your understanding.

Abide and remain until you are no longer in control of this relationship! Embrace this Word until you find yourself in the grip of the One who is much larger than anything you can take hold of.

So we looked at the first part of John 17:5 "...*abide in Me and My words abide in you*". The second part has such a significant sequence in the original Greek. It literally says: and you will desire, and you will ask, and it shall be created. Desire is the natural and inevitable consequence of abiding in Christ Jesus. His companionship, His conversation (word), stirs up desires, good and godly desires. The reason that He stirs these desires is not to disappoint you, but to fulfil you!

When you abide in Him, His word is going to develop these desires to such intensity that eventually you will not be able to keep quite ... you will ask. And your Father will delight in creating that for which you asked, because that request began as His desire! Through your friendship (abiding), His desire has become your desire. Your request is the most beautiful music to His ears as He hears how accurately you have understood Him, grasped His thoughts, perceived His intentions and expressed it in words. He delights in creating the fulfilment of such desires.

Our requests no longer have their origin in need, but in gratitude. That's why Paul says: "*Don't worry about anything, but in everything, through prayer and petition with thanksgiving, let your requests be made known to God.*" (Phil 4:6) Even our requests are based on gratitude!

We are so used to ending our prayers with 'Amen', but did you know that one of the most effective prayers, is one that starts with 'Amen'?

"*Whatever God has promised gets stamped with the Yes of Jesus. In him, this is what we preach and pray, the great Amen, God's Yes and our Yes together, gloriously evident. God affirms us, making us a sure thing in Christ, putting his Yes within us.*" 1 Cor 1:20-21 MSG

Discover what was given to you in Christ and simply respond with 'Yes, Amen'. There's another scripture somewhere that says: agree with God and be at peace. So many of Paul's prayers were simply asking that our eyes would be opened to the glorious riches that were given to us in Christ.

Amen!

More resources available at:

www.hearhim.net

To **download Music & Lyrics** go to:

http://hearhim.net/wordpress/music/

To **download books & literature** go to:

http://hearhim.net/wordpress/book-downloads/

To **subsribe to email notifications**, go to:

http://www.hearhim.net/phplist/?p=subscribe

For similar resources go to:

http://www.mirrorreflection.net/

CPSIA information can be obtained at www.ICGtesting.com
Printed in the USA
LVOW062043260313

326016LV00001B/5/P